The Girl on the Swings: Transparency

Terra Leigh

Terra Leigh

Cover photography by J. Scott Wilson & Terra Leigh
Overleaf artwork provided by M. Antoinette Adams
Editing Assistance by Faith Griffin

1st run released May 2022, Hampton Roads, Virginia
copyright ©2022 Terra L. Walker,   Terra Leigh
ISBN: 978-1-952773-59-4

Table of Contents

Prelude: Forward Momentum

Dedication

Silence.

To the Readers

Prelude: Forward Momentum

I swing back and forth
On this cold metal seat,
Hearing the creaks
Of the chains carrying me.

The wind rushes
Through my hair,
Strands clouding my view
Before clearing away.

An empty basketball court
Grows and shrinks before me,
And with the wind blowing,
I can hear a girl singing.

As I swing back,
She shrinks to that
Of a child.

But swinging forward,
She stands tall as
A confident woman.

Someone familiar...

Curiosity lifts my brow
As my hand reaches out,
Watching the girl mirror
My every move.

She is me,

Growing into a woman
Before shrinking back to a kid.

With each backwards movement,
I can see the child sadden,
Our hands never meeting once.

With each forward movement,
The adult brightens
As our fingers graze one another's.

Each forward swing brings me
Closer to the woman
I'm meant to be,

But never enough
To fully grasp her hand.

She continues to sing
As she watches me,
Keeping her hand outstretched
For mine.

She's waiting for me,
Ready to see me
Face to face.

And I'm ready to meet her...

One day,
The forward momentum
Of my swing will launch me,
Sending me into her arms.

I just need to push harder,
Work harder than the little girl
I was before.
Become stronger.

One day,
My forward momentum will
Send me soaring.

Dedication

To all those who have lost,
Are trying to protect,
Or who have yet to find
Their voice.

Silence.

A single spotlight
And a girl with a mic.

Every word may be dull,
May kill a mood,
May offend someone,

But she's spent eight years
Keeping everything inside.

It's time
To tell her story.

I

Creaking

AA

Hi,
My name is Terra.

I can speak two languages
But struggle to say hello.

I write poetry on my phone
But can't send a simple text.

I can take pictures of myself
But always tense up with video calls.

I'm automatically logged onto Facebook,
Scrolling the dashboard
Without making a post.

I think way too much,
Pouring anxieties
All over my daily routines.

I want to say
I'm sorry,
But Satan tells me
That's an empty plea for attention.

I'm too quiet for my own good.
Even my cat is shocked
When I speak to him,

And I run wild with daydreams
Forgetting where I stand.

I'm not in this meeting
For an alcohol addiction.

It's for my silence

That will one day
Kill me…

Transparency

You're not allowed to frown,

Not allowed to let
A single tear fall,
Or ball up your fists.

Don't even think
About complaining.
I guarantee
No one will listen.

Now yes,
You can scribble down
Your fears and worries,

But no one has time
To read them,

And if you need a shoulder
To steady yourself on,
This is the wrong place.

We don't have time
To listen to the station
Your emotions spit freely on,

Nor do we have time
To check on you.

It's time to work
And work
And work.

Girl,
You'll be working
'Til your skin pales
And goes slack.

Now then,

Stop picking at your lips
And get back to work.

Bike Riding

My uncle tried to teach me
How to ride a bike

The exact same way
He was taught:

Holding the back of the seat
While I pedaled,
Steadying me
As I picked up speed.

But, because I was different
From him
And "normal" kids at that age,

I had balance issues.

My bike careened to the left.
I high-fived a splinter so hard
It stuck into my hand.

Mom gave me a band-aid,
But I never got back on that bike,

Just like
I'll never go back
To the people and things
That hurt me now.

Caffeinated Rush

They clamor in,

Picking up their coffees
From the counter
Or straight to the register
With their phones.

No one ever sits down
Or closes their eyes
Or watches cars pass by.

They don't breathe,
Don't sit with themselves
And just be.

Technology creates
Too much convenience.
We have no more patience,
Seeking rush after rush.

But what happens
When the rush is gone?

Children See Everything

'Cause she needs no more stress,
They just smile
On the shelves
She picks them up from.

They never say a word
For someone to come save her.

They pray to God,
Flipping their pages,
Her shrinking self-esteem
Ripped to shreds,

And suffocating worries
From her negativity
Close their covers.

With each second she just sits there,
They bite their fingernails,

Watching tears warp the stained laminate,
Listening to her cries.

They hide
Behind thin covers.

A Beast

She screams.
Nails and bolts fling
As she rips doors
Off their hinges.

Oak shatters.
Flakes scatter
Across the kitchen.

The salad mix becomes a victim,
Decorating the floor.
Red cabbage dangles
Off the coat rack.

Mom's calling,
Grabbing,
Holding her back,

But she thrashes,
Smashes the glass on the stove.

All of this
In the walls of her brain

While she just cries at the sink.

Mother

She sees me
Working 10 to 5
Then driving to fencing
With no breaks.

She watches me
Carry fatigue
Up the front steps
When I finally get home.

She sits quietly
While I scribble in notebooks
Or type on my phone,

Not wanting another poem
To die.

She listens to my nails
Click against computer keys,
Hears the bangs of my fists
Punching walls in my stress.

She even watches me
Break into tears
While eating spaghetti,

Then drops all her work
To sit in the guest seat
Of a Patient First cubby
While a nurse checks
My panicking heartbeat.

She sees me.

She. Sees. Me.

To The Man Making Fun of My Music

Yes,
I listen to K-pop.

No,
I don't understand
What it says.

But the notes and lyrics
Slip into my ears so easily.

They take me on a tour
Of their feelings,
And I have so much fun.

It's like discovering
A new civilization or ruins
Under modern day living.

I have to come back for more.

Because under those
Indescribable syllables,
There are messages just for me.

I wish I could tell you
In person,

But I know
You'll just make fun of me.

Bathroom Saga (Part 1)

Each tear splashes
Against ceramic flooring.

The patters applaud
Her bravery
to pray to God for help,

Massage her shoulders
For what's to come next.

When she turns
The shower off
And steps out the tub,

Silence greets her.

Neck & Neck

It's a race
Between Praise and Anxiety!

Praise leaps
Over mountains of stress,
But Anxiety trips her
To take first place.

Praise is quick
To get back up
And close the gap,

Shoving Anxiety out of the way
To take the lead.

Did you see that?

Anxiety just grabbed Praise's shirt
And yanked her down!
But no fouls are called!

They're neck and neck
Through this girl's prayers
On the way to the finish line.

Winner gets control of this girl's mind
For the day.

Who's it gonna be??

For Once, I Won't Complain

You make me
Want to take this knife up
On its offer,

Let it caress my skin
In slow inches,
Poke my tender spots,

Let it admire
My ulna artery,
Stare at it deeply,

Press more and more
Until the sea of epidermis parts
To let it kiss the cord.

I won't tell anyone…

But this
Is one of those moments
I'm glad

God doesn't give me
What I want.

Symptoms of Anxiety

Rampant heartbeat,
Tight throat,
Shaky hands,
Wandering mind.

This is not me
High on caffeine.

It's a wall
Between me
And the right decision.

E.K.G.

Looking ahead,
Cursing Starbucks
For not curing me,

I stare at the speckled ceiling,

Barely feeling the wires
Draping my arms,
The plastic adhesive
Pinpointing my heart.

I'm trying to focus
On something
Other than my panic

Or this voice calling me
A failure,

I can't even hear Mom's conversation
About outvoting Trump…

The nurse looks at me,
Tells me nothing is wrong,
Except

I've got too much
Sitting on my heart.

Terra Leigh

Crunchy

I like my cereal crunchy,

Grains screaming
With every bite,
Submitting to my power
In sudden bursts of flavor.

It tastes better

And keeps me grounded
In the present.

I'm Tired

I.

It's 8am.
The alarm clock calls me.
I am just waking,

But my mind fights
To keep these relaxed eyes open.

All I do
Is check the weather,
And I want to go
Back to sleep.

II.

It's been 30 minutes
Since work started,

Only lesson planning,
Sitting in a silent cafeteria,
My mind creating scenarios
Based off the scriptures
I find on Pinterest.

III.

It's 6:30 in the evening.
I'm laying down in the sunroom
After a snack.

I close my eyes
For a nap,

But my mind won't stop talking,

Telling me
All of its ideas,
Flipping through its notes.

It reminds me
Of everything I've done
And what I still need to do.

It makes suggestions
Of what I could do next.

It's louder
Than the party
My neighbor holds
Every weekend.

I'm trying
To be its friend,

But sometimes,
I just want it
To shut up.

IV.

It's only 8pm.

I walk up to my mom
And tell her
I'm tired...

She still doesn't understand.

Bombing

Tick...

She tucks herself away
In her car
As her mother asks
Where she's going.

Tick...

She pulls off and drives.
No radio.
No music.

Tick, tick...

She ignores the landmarks,
The familiarity,
Pulls into an empty school lot.

Tick, tick, tick...

She rests her head
On the steering wheel,
And

Click!

Transparency

She screams.

Frustrations splatter
All over the wheel.
Debris drifts,
Lint in the dim-lit space,

A mess she won't let
Anyone else get caught in.

Please

Take her hand.

She knows no better,
Wandering the lobby
While you wait for coffee.

In one second,
She could be out that door
Her fingers keep pressing on,
And you won't see her again.

Please, take her hand.

She won't ask for yours,
Too stubborn
To admit her needs.

Please, take my hand.

I should never be left
Alone.

Blanket

Hold me
A little tighter.

You're the only one
Willing to give me a hug.

The Warnings

You know it's real
When you have to force food
Down your throat,

Take big gulps of water
To keep everything down,

And chew slowly
When you just want to swallow
And be done.

No desire to hydrate,
Staring at lined paper
With nothing to say.

You can't tell your mother
You're not hungry,

Just shrug your shoulders
At your favorite meal
Like it's garbage.

It's real
When you won't even pick up
Your favorite book,

When you want to ask for help
But can't.

When you want to tell
Your mother
About your problems,
But your lips clench shut.

It's real.

Opposites

My brain's encased
In a hard shell.

Every outside opinion
Ricochets into silence.

Nothing can scratch it.

But it's friends
With my heart,

A small girl
Opening up to everyone.

One shove
Leaves scratches
All over her body.

My brain calculates
Exit strategies
For the worst outcomes.

My heart carries hope
In all of her pockets.

They come together
And instantly start yelling
Over who is right.

Neither can agree.

So, on those days
I sit alone,
Not talking,

Please know
They are in
Another argument.

Clogging

Murky soap water
Stands over the drain.

She won't let these emotions out
So she can finally breathe.

II

Swinging

PTSD

Freshman year,
I thought I was spied on.

Secret bullies with too much free time,
They sought my tears
Through their jokes.

Their gossip walked
Through concrete walls.
I couldn't even study.

My body and grades shriveled
While time skipped away.

Ten years later,
The same condescending behavior
Has found new skin and voices,

And I've learned
I suffer from PTSD.

Profiles

He doesn't care about the work I've missed
Or the days I've been late
'Cause of his morning antics.

He mistakes my tears for joy,
And every time I walk away,
He yanks me back by my curls.

I'm not a victim…
I can break his fingers.

I'm not a victim…
I can stab him with these pens.

I'm not a victim…

I don't want to be a victim,

But I can't pull free
From his grasp,

Can't spell out my problems
In simple English
Or dial 911 for help.

Terra Leigh

Please,
Don't call me
A victim.

Please,
Don't throw me
Your pity.

Why won't one of you
Stop staring
And get me
Some help?

While I'm Here

I love thunderstorms,

Especially when the wind builds,
And leaves lose their bearings.
A chair may topple over,
And lightning finally touches Earth.

It's just the release of humidity,

But I think God is adding
A little spark
To mediocre weather.

It's how He makes sure
We're listening,
Testing our patience
When we can't follow
Regular routines.

Even He can't resist
A little fun,
Depicting beauty with chaos.

Which is why
I sit at the window and watch,
Despite mom's complaints.

When we get to heaven,
We won't see anything like this
Again.

Squeezing

She swipes her card,
Types the zip code,
Waits for permission
To lift the nozzle.

She selects the grade
And squeezes
Halfway to halfway,

Just enough for the numbers
To tick slowly,

To get what she needs
Without the excess air,

The nozzle whining
Under the need
To practice restraint,

Like me

When I'm so stressed
But clench my fists
And retreat from others
So I don't complain,

Forcing myself
To practice self-control
'Cause no one else will keep me
Accountable.

Seething words
Don't make a difference,

Not in this world.

Storm Mode

We make a big deal
Of hurricanes,

Lifting furniture,
Stacking sandbags over doors.

We take pictures
Of our possessions,
Hide curriculum
In our attics.

Some people evacuate
To higher grounds,
And the news stays on
The entire day.

But what do we do
When a person's emotions
Surge over our expectations?

Why can't we take
The same precautions?

And since we can't control
The weather,
Why can't we take the initiative

To stop someone's personal disaster?

This Should Not Be an Answer

She stares at the knife,
The plastic bottle,
The wine glass,

All willing
To show her reflection,
To dive deep down
And listen to her heartbeat
When no one else will.

And she smiles
Through overwhelming tears,

Ready to fall
Into their embrace
And rest…

Promise Me

These tears are temporary,

Your vocal cords
Won't blow
From all the yelling,

No blood will show
After punching air.

Promise me

The stars won't die
In your eyes,
And light will still shine
From your gapped smile,

You will always
Pick up your pencil
And write,

Record your dreams
Waiting to be accomplished.

Promise me

You won't drown
Your family in silence,
Won't push them away,

Worship will be
Your remedy,
Daily showers will be
Baptisms,

Rejections
Won't be crucifixions,
The knife will stay
In your imagination,

And you'll stop saying
No one likes you
And start carrying yourself.

Promise me

When you wake up,
You'll still see me.
I'm always right here.

Promise me.

Terra Leigh

Blessed Acceptance

She fights battles
With eyes closed,
Grinding teeth,
And clogging words.

She fights
Mumbling His name,
A choked plea
Grating against her circumstances.

She fights in tears
'Cause there's someone
Loving enough
To be her shield,

Cast her fears away
With a single wave,
And a kiss on her forehead,

Shush her sobs
And tell her
Everything will be okay.

She fights with a smile,
Singing to an invisible man
Who wraps her in golden robes of acceptance
And whispers her name
In reassurance.

She doesn't need anything else.

I'm Maturing

My cat, Tink,
Likes to charge at me
When he wants to play
And toddles off like a giggling child
As I chase him.

When I pick up a toy,
After one throw,
He scampers off to eat.

He has never hurt me,

'Til one evening
When I fed his curiosity,

Lifted him up
So he could see my mom
Chiseling ice out of the freezer chest.

He wiggled,
And I tried to set him down.

But he lost it,
Claws digging into my hands.

He walked up to me
After I dressed the wounds,
Brushed against my leg,
And purred an apology.

Now,
I know what I said earlier,
But

There's something
I'll go back to
Even if it hurts me.

"Do Not Be Afraid"

Appears in the Bible
365 times,

But what does God say
On that extra day
Of a leap year?

Thick Lines

My lips are a sealed vault.

It starts with the family,
Generations of people
Carrying stress on their backs,

Pretending
To be okay.

It moves to the public,
Four years as
A social outcast,

Going to classes,
Singing in choir,
Then retreating to my room
For the rest of the night,

People hearing
But never listening,

My quiet character
Setting me apart for good.

You see,
As much as I want
To get close to someone,
I draw thick lines of privacy.

So many
That people don't want
To attempt crossing,

So many
That my family can't find the stress
Behind my smile,

So many
That even God
Has a hard time
Believing my prayers.

Today,

I walked up to my mom
And admitted my fears.

She couldn't say anything.

Tenacious Tales

His aim is not my appearance.

Instead,
He shoots right at my heart,

Aiming for the confidence
In my character
And the assurance in my dreams.

He hits the kneecaps
Of my thoughts
That I can be accepted,

Scratches my trust in God.
Each flake is sour,

But I never stop.

Bruised and bloody,
I keep walking,
Using battle tales
To feed others.

If I don't survive this,
At least they will know
What to look out for.

Not Your Average Rapunzel

She sits atop a tower,
Gazing out the only window,
Singing about Freedom,
The person she has yet to meet.

But she is no princess,

Loading lead bullets
Into pencils,
Aligning her paper.

Each written word's a shot
Through the dark,
Through her fears,

To what she dreams of.

This hard work
Will twist into the escape rope
She needs
To finally climb down,

One long strand
At a time.

In The Clearing

No one approaches.
No police investigations.

In the center
Of splattered emotions,
There she is,
Coughing up smoke.

Her fingers tremble,
Her feet numb.
Her bottom lip quivers.

Out of the people
Eavesdropping through their windows,
Only He braves the debris,

Doesn't ask
What happened,
Doesn't toss her advice,

Just wipes the ash off
With a soft rag,
Picks her up,
And carries her back home.

Once she looks
Into His eyes,

All she can do is smile.

Social Media

Is not my friend.

Its silence crushes
My self-esteem,
And it never confirms
My message deliveries.

It doesn't load
All the time,
And people expect
Too much attention.

It laughs at the few
Likes I get,
Doesn't show my posts
On everyone's boards.

But I keep trying,

Keep uploading videos,
Posting and reposting.
I keep commenting,
Liking, and reblogging.

I keep speaking
With no replies

'Cause my light stretches,
Transmitting through the internet,
Passing the static of memes and politics

Just to get to you.

One day,
All my words
Will get to you.

Tetris

I draw my expectations
In the air,
Hoping they will float,

But they always pile up
On my face.

If I draw them
In the right places,
Maybe they will fall
Exactly where I need them to,

To clear this clutter of doubts.

Why I Don't Get Excited

It's easier
To meet Reality
Face to face

Than to jump
From my home of expectations

And try to land
On both feet.

I Never Learned How to Speak

When I was little,
Some kid tried to take my chips
And all I did was clench a fist.

In high school,
People made fun of my hair,
But I just turned away.

Some kids found my lyrics
And started talking.
I sank into my seat
Until I found my confidence.

College was a battleground.
More days than others,
I was the foreign exchange student
People pointed and laughed at.

When I spoke to RAs and counselors,
None of my words fully translated.

Instead of attacking,
I hid myself in earbuds
And music.

No one understood.

I never mastered the English language,
All the slang and nuances.

Even now,
I let my helping hands
And facial expressions
Be my tell-all.

I stick close
To people I trust,
And my silence is a punch to the gut.

Momma says
I'm wearing my heart on my sleeve,
But honestly,
It's the only way

I know how to speak.

VT Expressions

The first time
I read poetry
Was in college.

TAB, Rone, and Dxtr
Cheered me on
From the sidelines

When all I could think about
Was how my words were
Discarded loose change,

Especially after
I was a pin cushion
For mental and verbal abuse
Freshman year.

Singing is easy.
My voice is an instrument
In God's band.

But that night,
He edged me
Into taking that pen
And signing my name,

Letting the words
Flow like fresh paint
Onto people's walls.

My anxiety took a seat
For five minutes,

Awestruck
By the strength
She was only trying to protect.

From that day on,
There has been
No going back.

I'm The One

Lifting boulders.
Her weight training
Goes to lifting papers
And turning the ignition.

I play doctor
While she rests,
Deciphering her groans into needs.

I get her out of bed,

Wash her,
Dress her,
Feed her.

She always asks
To meet in the bathroom
So she doesn't have to ask
For help in front of others.

Despite her strong voice
And knowing what she wants,
Determination fades from her eyes.

The fire I stoked
Grows dimmer
With each rejection letter.

Transparency

She festers in her own tears,
But only I can smell the stench.

I've read the farewell letters
Tucked in boot boxes,
Crumpled and thrown them away.

I've given her space to work,
Shushed the crowds,
Promoted her.

I get on my hands and knees,
Scrubbing the gunk off her heart
And feed her encouragement
Through my songs.

Today,
She calls me again,

But this time,

She's waiting for me
Outside the door.

Terra Leigh

Fall in Line

They want it,

The scrunched eyebrows,
The gritting teeth,
The deep sighs.

They want you
To return to your office
And complain,

Carry them on your back
To meet your family in rants

And come in the next morning
With aching shoulders and baggy eyes
From them haunting your dreams.

You've already fallen
Into their line,

Hiking their stress
On your shoulders
From 9 to 5,

The failed communication,
Trips back and forth
From your desk,

The meetings
That go well over
The minutes mentioned.

But take a deep breath,

Drop their weight
And step to the side.

Don't even look at them
As you turn around.

Keep your back straight,
Body relaxed
As you find

Your own paradise.

Traveling

Military movers,
Families,
Corporate offices,
Schools and buses.

Smack dab in the middle,
I wander the walls,

Humming my own tune
Against the traffic horns,
Finding the holes
Where performance plays.

I do my duty in the day.
Use the nights to play with God's gifts.

And for once,
I speak my wish
In a crowded restaurant,
Through a single mic,

And everyone in the room
Points to you.

For once, I can finally breathe.
No matter my fear, I keep moving.
I'm dropping the dollars needed for this first step,
And I'm not crying.

'Cause here, I have found life,
Found a place my words belong
Here, the traffic stops,
And the mundane parts just for me.

And I haven't taken
A look back.

Driving I-81

Mountains run beside me.
Trees wave in the breeze.
Korean and Japanese
Belt from the speakers.

We drive alone,
Your Holy Spirit filling
The empty passenger seat,

Me singing every note,
Every memorized word
While you listen.

Last week,
I cried until
I remembered how to breathe,
My seams bursting open
In a Patient First,

Your hand unable
To pass my wall of stress,
Unable to remind me
That I need no one else.

Today,
I can't hold your hand,
Can't look into your eyes
Through any of the mirrors.

But thank you
For staying with me
In these moments.

Dear 2019,

You broke me,

Ripping Japan and future jobs
From my hands,
Breaking promises
I keep sprawled out in memories.

All that's left
Is a 28-year-old girl
Not knowing where to go.

But, at least,
I'm holding God's hand.

III

The Leap

T-E-R-R-A

I went to Tapioca Go and ordered
A large peach green tea
With mango jelly.

The lady at the register
Asked for my name,
And I told her it was
Terra.

She asked me,
"How do you spell it?
T-a-r-a?"

And, well,
I almost lost it.

You see,
Not many people
Ask how I spell my name.

They stick to their own perceptions
Not ready for correction,
Lumping me into the same pile
As everyone else.

I can never find keychains
Specifically for me.

Those Facebook posts with names
Never include mine.

I was surprised
When my exact name
Showed up on Santa's Nice List
Last year.

My mother wanted me
To be different.

She made sure
I'd be different.
When you hear *Terra Leigh*,
Only my face should pop up.

So, I spelled it out for her,

And for the first time
In a long time,
I heard someone finally say,

"Oh! I like that spelling.
It's very unique."

Wild

I don't fit
Into any of society's pegs.
I speak a different dialect.

I love staying home,
Reading and writing.
Swinging a sword is my exercise.

My Pinterest is full
Of Japan pics,
Favorite bands, and anime.

I have a board
Dedicated to tiny homes
And one solely for God.

I drive 40+ minutes
To support my friends,
And the emotional door is always open.

I cannot lie.
I will not lie.
Honesty has become a middle name.

I know what
My future should look like,
Been chasing dreams since third grade.

And my eyes may wander,
But I never get sidetracked.

I am a rare breed,
Fashioned to stand
Outside the norm.

So, society calls me,
"Wild."

28

She needs to be
More independent,
Have her own apartment
And a steady job.

She needs to stop
Searching for acceptance letters
In other people's reactions,

Stop following
Her favorite artists
For inspiration,

Stop clinging
To big dreams
In a narrow world,

Trash her childish charm,
Look adults in the eyes
Instead of bending
To talk to their egos.

She needs to be more,

But she's found
Leaning against His shoulder,

Transparency

Singing with eyes closed,
Writing with headphones on,
Reading and reading and reading.

She doesn't hear
Anything we say…

I think
We need to be
More carefree
Like her.

I Am a Failure

Sown together
With a kind heart,
Cautious mind,
And elegant words.

But this body has eyes
That only see my reflection,

Ears stained
By behind-the-back insults,
Bruises all over my character.

I am a failure,

But that doesn't mean
I'm worthless.

'Cause God still helps me
Out of bed
And gives me work to do.

He still speaks to me
And gives me time
To calm down
From my anxieties.

Transparency

He waits for me
To see my flaws
So He can turn them to gold.

Yes,
I'm a failure,

But I'm still loved.

Never Pray in Front Of Mirrors

She surrenders
To the Holy Spirit,

Strides around the bathroom
With arms raised,
Overflowing rivers
Of praise and petition flooding.

She stops at the mirror
And opens her eyes,

Crescents shifting
To full moons,

Fortes shrinking
To pianos,

Conversations drifting
To silence.

And she stares
At the woman on the other side
Who stares back,

Both too in awe with the other
To do anything else.

Technology is Amazing!

I can swipe cards
On my phone
To ring up books,
And the money goes straight
To my bank account.

If I drew on my tablet,
Every move could be mirrored
To pinpointed locations.

I can save poems
On my laptop
And open them on a desktop
In a different house.

But technology can't imitate

That drag of pencils against paper
When the lead reaches the barrel,
Plastic or wood scraping the surface.

It can't remake
The summoning of small wind
With each page flip,
The relieved sigh the bind makes,

And it'll never have that smell,
That freshness,
That newness,

Or carry the weight
Of filled, marked pages.

Technology is amazing,

But I'll stick with
The old school methods.

Joy

You're a leaf
Easily swept away
When the wind plays
With my hair.

You're stepped on
With a sudden change in tone
Or forgotten manners.

You're crushed
By my overthinking,
Rejections from others,
Even being forced
To go through the drive thru.

But you're so heavy

That I know
The exact moment
You're gone,

And my entire day
Is a mess
Of routine notions.

It's a battle,
Keeping something
So fleeting,

But I'm ready.

Fire

They warned me
To never play with fire.

So, I watched it
From a distance,
Let the heat graze my skin.

I'd watch it burn bright,
Determined to keep the house warm,
Watch it change clothes
Depending on what it mixed with.

I'd light a match
Just to see how close
It would trail to my fingers.

I even watched it gobble
My garage down
'Cause no one was paying attention.

I've watched it crackle
In the night sky,
Sometimes, in a person's eyes,

And I hear it grow
In focused voices.

Terra Leigh

I inhaled it from others.
Now, it rises and falls in my chest.

I'm an adult now.

So, I can make
My own rules.

On The Strip

I've gotta deal
With the real world,

Learn its patterns,
Get used to its speed,
Go off the line
To hit it simultaneously.

I've gotta play right,

Lure it in
With perfectly timed fakes,
Pull away and parry
As soon as it cuts.

I've gotta be patient,

Steady advances,
Tempo changes,
Close in the distance
And strike with a swift swipe.

I've gotta keep going.

And when it realizes
What I've done,
I'll already be saluting.

I've won the bout.

Because of Him

Fear drives nails
Into my palms,
Into my ankles.

I'm hung by insecurities,
Crowned with anxieties.

Love trickles from the cuts.
Peace withers to nothing
As my teeth grind together.

People stare at me
Like I'm an alien.
Some can't see my wounds.

Some laugh,
Chilling my aged grief
To drink with their steak.

But this pain is nothing
Compared to what
My Brother suffered,

Physical humiliation
Despite His innocence,
Accepting the cruel fate
Our Father wrote for Him.

This is only a taste,

And if He can come back
Three days later
Looking like nothing happened,
Then I can stand as well,

Shed the world
Off my shoulders,
Wear the new body
I've been given.

It's all because of Him.

Back to My Prayers

I woke up this morning
With ten tons of emptiness
Resting on my chest.

I flailed through memories,
Trying to find where I went wrong,

Buried my face in Scriptures,
Closed my eyes in the shower and prayed.

But…

I'll take this
Over the numbing,

Over not knowing
That there's something
God needs to tweak,

Over the defeat,
Staring at my life
Like it's a threatening blank sheet
Of paper.

So, excuse me,

I've got to get back
To my prayers.

Roaring Run

Rushing water roars
Through my senses.

I'm the timid girl
Stepping out into the falls,
Washed of Fame's greed.

Each drop is a kiss
Sent by God,
Feathering my face
In congratulations.

It's a celebration
On a still spring day.

Gallery

Art is loved,

An idea crafted
By someone too enamored
To keep it in their head.

So, they block off time,
Let it manifest,
Let it breathe,

Nurture it
Until it walks on its own
With other people.

They watch the interactions,
How it's seen,
Heard,
Touched,

How it speaks
When no one listens,
Dances
When no one watches,
Sings
When no one comes.

Which is why
We are here,

Breaths mingling,
Eyes meeting,
Voices peeking out,

An art show

With a bountiful supply
To admire.

Lifeguard Duty

They trample
Over your weak body,
Scoffing
As you reach up for help.

There's no thinking
Of others
Before yourself,

And you are caught
In the waves
Of the world's selfishness.

But I see you.

I know your pain,
And I'm running straight to you,
Stringing words together
To toss out.

I hope you'll grab hold.

Classroom Antics

He waits for me
Around the corner,
Scares me
With sudden thoughts.

He sits next to me
And continues his hypotheses,
Shushed whispers no one catches.

He threatens me with worries
In the cafeteria.
My lunch becomes less appealing.

I run to one of my teachers,
Tell them what happened.
The best he gets is ISS.

He's quiet,
His best behavior,
Just to divert their attention,

Only for a few weeks
Before the cycle starts over.

I can't touch him.

My straightforward approach
Would get me in trouble.

But once my principal,
God, turns His back,

And I punch this brat
Right in the stomach
With blunt words and prayers.
Then, a swift right to his arm.

He sulks
As the bell rings,
Doesn't follow me out.

I am
Victorious.

Spoken Word Poetry

Is overflowing emotions
Repeated over and over
So people finally get it.

It's those people locked away
From society,
Stretching their legs
In the only place
They're accepted,

Longwinded,
A kite fluttering in night air,
Its tail dancing

Carefree
To the trees it could
Fly into.

It's the beauty
Of letting go
In a world that teaches
To hold on.

Everything
I wish I could do.

So, I'll sit
And listen to these artists
Spit words to life.

My ears will be
A place
Where they
Are always welcomed.

This Is

A lion's roar,
A train's horn,
A gushing waterfall.

This is
An explosion,
Fireworks in the sky,
The New Year's Ball dropping.

This is
A door kicked open,
Walls knocked down,
Homes bulldozed.

This is her
Finding her voice,

And she can't be stopped.

The Swing

It creaks
Back and forth,

Calling me to return
To its safe arms,

To play seesaw with the sky
As the woman in front of me walks away,

To forget the world.

But my butt stings
From sitting and watching
The world pass by.

So, I jump off.

And the swing
Creaks back and forth,
Rattling in the momentum,

Cheering me on
To keep going forward.

Terra Leigh

I Am a Temple

My eyes are
Stained glass windows
Catching the sun.

My hands are seats
To hold people.

These ears are soundproof walls
Absorbing every secret.

But lately,
Bitterness piles
In small patches.

I never noticed
'Til I looked inside
To see the covered crevices.

Temples can't clean
Themselves.

So, I've looked all over
For someone to take care of this mess,

Friends in far off places,
Silence in my room.

I even looked to the people
Who opened my doors to all of this.

But there's only one man
With the right experience,

Who can slip down
To every nook and cranny
And polish everything.

I got the number
From my neighbor.
I'm dialing it now.

The calendar's ready
To schedule His appointment.

One day,
This place
Will look like home again.

Free Will

She opens the door,
Steps aside and lets You in.

You'll ask what's wrong,
And she'll show
Every leaky faucet,
Every loose and lost screw.

Her words will quiver,
Emotions caught
In a crescendoing earthquake
As she repeats every step
Taken to get here,

All the YouTube videos,
Tumblr posts,
And what just made sense.

Tears will drop from her eyes
In her confession,
Knowing she can't do this alone,

And You'll smile,
Hands taking the payment
That is her clasped submission.

You'll take her hands
And say thank you.

She has finally chosen You.

Balancing Act

I watched a man drive
With a Hardee's cup
Riding on his truck's bumper.

Through every twist and turn,
It never flinched,
Didn't wobble driving over manholes
Or stopping at red lights.

Then, the truck took a sharp left,
And the cup went flying.

This is me
When I'm with you,
Fastened to firm beliefs
Before you send a surprise.

But I get back on my feet,
Pick up my spilled insides,
Dust myself off,

And you're right there,
Idling,
So I can get up
For another ride.

Unlikely Neighbor

I'm so used to living with you,
Anxiety.

Normal days,
My heart jumps rope
In my chest
Over small decisions.

I can't sit still
With my brain running
Tiny laps in this confining skull.

I go from appointment to appointment
With no breaks
Just to pay the bills
While still chasing poetry.

Peace is the next-door neighbor
I only wave to.

But one day,
He comes for a visit
While you're gone,
Bringing muffins and coffee.

Terra Leigh

We sit and talk,
And for once,
I don't have to keep
My guard up.

Since then,
He fills the gaps of my silence
Just by resting on the couch.

He lets me read
All I want
Wednesdays and Fridays
When work is done.

I can sit and watch
Netflix shows
Without him bugging me
That I'm not getting anything accomplished.

And he listens
When I finally find
Something to say.

I willingly fall
Into his embrace,
And we take naps
In the sunroom.

You can call me a cheater,
Even unfaithful.

It's fine.

Anxiety,
Our relationship
Is already over.

Bathroom Saga (Part 2)

I baptized myself today,

Dunked my head
Under shower water
And started praying.

The words were a river
Flowing over my life,
Washing the guilt off my body
And rinsing reluctant tears.

I closed my eyes
And reached up
To be in my Father's arms.

When I turned off the water,
I was singing

And finally felt
Embraced.

People Think I'm Crazy
for Going to So Many Open Mics

Streetlights greet me
As mom drives.

Signals guide me
To this stage,
This mic,

The restaurant tables
Clothed in white,
And to the wooden cat
Who accompanies all on stage,

Even to the bright coffee shops
Where other guests talk so loud
You can hear them
From the other side of the building.

I want to close my eyes
And meet Nap Time
For a few minutes,

But I'm the college student
Too excited to return home
For Fall Break

Terra Leigh

Here, a family
Of poets, singers, and entertainers,
Welcomes me
With a space of my own.

Conversations

Yes,
I talk to myself.

I close my eyes
And mouth conversations.

I walk in stores
And ask an invisible partner
If I should buy new pants.

I stop singing
To let my lips pray
At breaking speeds.

Yes,
That's me,
Just talking in my car
With no passengers.

And yes,
You can hear me
Mumbling through
The bathroom walls.

I know who lives
Inside this body.

And, for once,
I wanna talk.

A Child of God

I'm no longer a slave to fear.
I am a child of God.
I'm no longer a slave to fear.
I am a child of God.

He is the child
No one wants to be
Friends with,

Can't keep his hands
From leaving scratches.
His shouts bruise self-esteem,

And he snatches joy
With whispers
That we'll have no friends.

Every day
Is the same torture.

My silence is a curse,

But mother can be heard
Singing that song from church,

I'm no longer a slave to fear.
I am a child of God.

I'm no longer a slave to fear.
I am a child of God.

He says our words
Are dumpster food.
Our singing is worse
Than ground chestnuts.

He pulls us away from others,
Leaves indents
All over our hearts.

He hits us
When no one's looking,
Corners us
On the playground.

There's only so much
We can take,
Only so much
We can complain,
And mom sees my weathered smile.

So, she keeps singing,

I'm no longer a slave to fear.
I am a child of God.
I'm no longer a slave to fear.
I am a child of God.

The steps of this new day
Are shaky,
Anxious.

But when he comes,
We turn,

Attention directed
On dreams of friendship,
Obtaining purpose in efforts
Whether the world watches or not.

And as we step away from his threatening advances,
We smile and start singing
My mom's favorite song,

I'm no longer a slave to fear.
I am a child of God.
I'm no longer a slave to fear.
I am a child of God.

The Coronation

I'm making a crown
Out of dreams conceived
When I scribbled wavy lines on paper,

Out of fairy tales constructed
With my favorite characters.

I'm weaving these strands together
With love letters tucked away or burned,

High school side eyes
And tears punched out by rejections
That haunt me even now.

I fortify this creation
With coats of God's wisdom,

Sand down the rough edges
With His love,
And paint the whole thing
In His peace.

This crown is my right of passage
Up to my throne.

Paper Planes

These books are paper planes
Thrown one after another.

I may be horrible
At the throw
And the construction,

But they still fall
Onto someone's lap,
Still reach close destinations.

And one day,
They will soar
Over rivers, oceans, and deserts,

Bringing smiles and confidence
To whoever reads them.

I've Learned to Open My Lips

To let words pour
Like an open faucet,

To let my emotions take flight
Through the skies,
Into ears,
Into hearts.

I've learned to let hands
Transpose my words to script,
Sending it out to everyone.

I've learned to tell silence
To take a backseat,

Hear what I say,
Watch what I do,
See the growth
In a small woman.

I've learned how to be me.

Now,
To see
Who will listen.

Called On

When you don't know
What to say,
Raise your hand high.

Someone is always watching.

And when they pick on you,
Start from the beginning.

Tell them your birthday
And the stories your mother repeats,
Like how you scribbled on paper
Before you knew what words looked like
And read the newspaper upside down.

Your favorite shows were
Ranma and Sailor Moon,
And fictional characters stole your heart
Before you knew what love was.

Tell them how you didn't eat meat
Unless it was deer,
How ZoeGirl was your favorite band,
And you actually liked going to school.

Tell them how you were laughed at
For writing lyrics,
How your sixth-grade teacher
Read your notebooks,

Unable to believe
You were just writing.

Tell them you were an overachiever
With few friends
But could still do fine
On your own.

Reminisce over the guys you liked,
How they rejected you
One at a time,

But you still kept walking.

Testify of how life has been
A constant battle,
How standing in God's presence is nerve wrecking,
And you're scared of getting what you want.

Just keep narrating
Up to the time
They called on you.

Terra Leigh

Then stop.
Let them breathe.

Those worth keeping
Will have stayed
For your whole story.

To The Readers,

First and foremost, thank you for reading this book.

Just as "E.K.G." read, I have kept a lot on my heart.

With unconscious encouragement from some of my friends and artists I look up to, I started to dive into my own life story. Though it took me a bit longer to get to this point, there's still a lot I struggle with now. God had some stuff He wanted me to put out first.

I hope this book is a good example and encourages others to speak up about their own troubles. Not just to be transparent but to also find the good qualities in your character. The healing process is long, but this is a start.

This is just one chapter in my life.
I hope it encourages you to find your own support system or healthy ways to cope, even if it's just prayers to God and jotting everything down in a journal. Someone will be there to listen.

Thank you!
-Terra Leigh

Colophon

Brought to you by Wider Perspectives Publishing, care of James Wilson, with the mission of advancing the poetry and creative community of Hampton Roads, Virginia.
This page used to have many cute and poetic expressions, but the sheer number of quality artists deserving mention has superseded the need to art. This has become some serious business; please check out how *They art...*

Nick Marickovich
Grey Hues
Madeline Garcia
Chichi Iwuorie
Symay Rhodes
Tanya Cunningham-Jones
        (Scientific Eve)
Raymond M. Simmons
Samantha Borders-Shoemaker
Taz Weysweete'
Jade Leonard
Darean Polk
Bobby K.
        (The Poor Man's Poet)
J. Scott Wilson (TEECH!)
Charles Wilson
Gloria Darlene Mann
Neil Spirtas
Jorge Mendez & JT Williams
Sarah Eileen Williams
Stephanie Diana (Noftz)
Shanya – Lady S.
Jason Brown (Drk Mtr)
Ken Sutton
Crickyt J. Expression
Se'Mon-Michelle Rosser

Lisa M. Kendrick
Cassandra IsFree
Nich (Nicholis Williams)
Samantha Geovjian Clarke
Natalie Morison-Uzzle
Gus Woodward II
Patsy Bickerstaff
Edith Blake
Jack Cassada
Dezz
Catherine TL Hodges
Kent Knowlton
Linda Spence-Howard
Tony Broadway
Zach Crowe
Mark Willoughby
Martina Champion
... and others to come soon.

the Hampton Roads
        Artistic Collective
        (757 Perspectives) &
The Poet's Domain
are all WPP literary journals in cooperation with Scientific Eve or Live Wire Press

Check for those artists on FaceBook, Instagram, the Virginia Poetry Online channel on YouTube, and other social media.

Hampton Roads Artistic Collective is an extension of WPP which strives to simultaneously support worthy causes in Hampton Roads and the local creative artists.

Made in the USA
Middletown, DE
23 August 2022

71080781R00076